THE ALL-TIME GREATEST
LOVESONGS

This publication is not authorised for sale in the
United States of America and/or Canada.

WISE PUBLICATIONS
London/New York/Paris/Sydney/Copenhagen/Madrid

Exclusive Distributors:
MUSIC SALES LIMITED
8/9 Frith Street,
London W1V 5TZ, England.
MUSIC SALES PTY LIMITED
120 Rothschild Avenue,
Rosebery, NSW 2018,
Australia.

Order No. AM957900
ISBN 0-7119-7345-8
This book © Copyright 1999 by Wise Publications

Designed by Chloe Alexander.
Compiled by Peter Evans.

YOUR GUARANTEE OF QUALITY:
As publishers, we strive to produce every book to the highest
commercial standards. This book has been carefully designed to
minimise awkward page turns and to make playing from it a real
pleasure.
Particular care has been given to specifying acid-free, neutral-sized
paper made from pulps which have not been elemental chlorine
bleached. This pulp is from farmed sustainable forests and was
produced with special regard for the environment. Throughout, the
printing and binding have been planned to ensure a sturdy, attractive
publication which should give years of enjoyment.
If your copy fails to meet our high standards, please inform us and we
will gladly replace it.

Music Sales' complete catalogue describes thousands of titles and is
available in full colour sections by subject, direct from Music Sales
Limited. Please state your areas of interest and send a cheque/postal
order for £1.50 for postage to: Music Sales Limited, Newmarket Road,
Bury St. Edmunds, Suffolk IP33 3YB.

ALL I HAVE TO GIVE

WORDS & MUSIC BY FULL FORCE

Verse 2:
When you talk does it seem like he's not
Even listening to a word you say?
That's okay babe, just tell me your problems
I'll try my best to kiss them all away
Does he leave when you need him the most?
Does his friends get all your time?
Baby please – I'm on my knees
Praying for the day that you'll be mine

But my love is all I have to give *etc.*

BABY CAN I HOLD YOU?

WORDS & MUSIC BY TRACY CHAPMAN

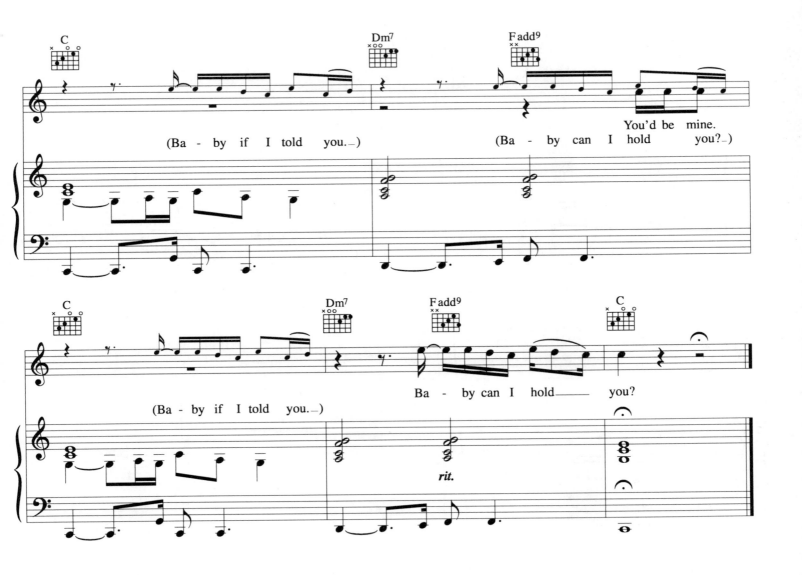

Verse 2:
Forgive me is all that you can't say
Years gone by and still
Words don't come easily
Like forgive me, forgive me.

Verse 3:
I love you is all that you can't say
Years gone by and still
Words don't come easily
Like I love you, I love you.

CAN YOU FEEL THE LOVE TONIGHT

(FROM WALT DISNEY PICTURES' "THE LION KING")

MUSIC BY ELTON JOHN. WORDS BY TIM RICE

CARELESS WHISPER

WORDS & MUSIC BY GEORGE MICHAEL & ANDREW RIDGELEY

I feel so ___ un ___ sure ___
Time can nev ___ er mend ___
To-night the mu - sic seems so loud, ___ I

To Coda ⊕

20

EACH TIME

WORDS & MUSIC BY BRIAN HARVEY, JOHN HENDY, TERRY COLDWELL, MARK REID, IVOR REID & JON BECKFORD

(I said you blow my mind.)   (Oh yeah   ooh)   1. Have you

heard of a say - ing   that those who are pay - ing?   You don't
(Verse 2 see block lyric)

know what you got ___ till it's gone. ___   Well

there was my call - ing   I knew I was fall - ing in - to

23

some-thing that would— be so wrong.— But I got hold of my-self— and

changed for the bet - ter, I can't— get you out— of my mind,—

'cause some-thing in - side— made

me re - al - ise— you were fine.— (Each time when we're a -

Verse 2:
I know from this feeling inside there's a feeling
I know that I'm in control
Every day I am yearning, this love I feel burning
Burning right through my soul
So let's make the start
Of something that cannot be broken
The mould is so strong
Treat this love as a child
Then grows into something worthwhile.

Each time when we're alone *etc.*

(EVERYTHING I DO) I DO IT FOR YOU

WORDS BY BRYAN ADAMS & ROBERT JOHN 'MUTT' LANGE. MUSIC BY MICHAEL KAMEN

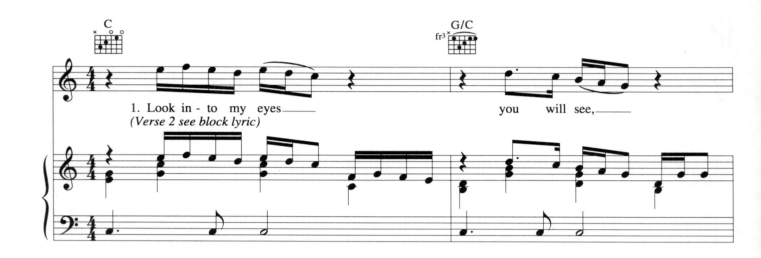

1. Look in-to my eyes___ you will see,___
(Verse 2 see block lyric)

what you mean to___ me. Search your heart,___ search your

soul,___ and when you find me there you'll search___ no more. Don't

tell me it's not worth try-in' for, you can't tell me it's not worth dy-in'

for. You know it's true,_____ ev-ery-thing I do, I do it for—

you.   There's

no love   like   your love   and   no   oth - er   could give

29

more love, there's no-where unless you're there all the

time, all the way yeah.

1. **2.**

Oh you can't

tell me it's not worth fight-ing for, I can't help it, there's no-thin' I want more. Yeah I would

Verse 2:
Look into your heart
You will find there's nothin' there to hide
Take me as I am, take my life
I would give it all, I would sacrifice.

Don't tell me it's not worth fightin' for
I can't help it, there's nothin' I want more
You know it's true, everything I do
I do it for you.

EVERY TIME I CLOSE MY EYES

WORDS & MUSIC BY BABYFACE

ev - 'ry time I close my eyes I thank the Lord that I've— got

you,— and you've got me too.— And ev-'ry time I think of it, I

pinch my-self 'cause I don't be - lieve it's true, that some-one like you— loves— me

too.—

some-one like you___ loves me too.___ To think of all the nights I've cried my-self to sleep, ___ you real-ly ought to know how much you mean___ to me, ___ it's on-ly right that you be in my life right here with me. Oh, ba-by, ba-by.

Verse 2:
Girl, I think that you are truly something, yes you are.
And you're, you're every bit of a dream come true.
With you babe, it never rains and it's no wonder
The sun always shines when I'm near you.
It's just a blessing that I have found somebody like you.

FROM THIS MOMENT ON

WORDS & MUSIC BY SHANIA TWAIN & ROBERT JOHN 'MUTT' LANGE

GOTHAM CITY

WORDS & MUSIC BY ROBERT KELLY

1. I'm look-ing ov-er the sky-line of ____ the ci-ty, ____
2. Sleep-ing a-wake be-cause of fear,

how loud, quiet nights in the midst of crime.
how children are drowning in their tears.

How next door to happiness lives sorrow and
How we need a place where we can go, and

signals of solution in the sky.
then when ev'ryone will have a hero

A city of just-

-ice, a city of love, a city of peace

I BELIEVE I CAN FLY

WORDS & MUSIC BY ROBERT KELLY

Verse 2:
See I was on the verge of breaking down,
Sometimes silence can seem so loud.
There are miracles in life I must achieve,
But first I know it stops inside of me.

Oh, if I can see it,
Then I can be it.
If I just believe it,
There's nothing to it.

I WILL ALWAYS LOVE YOU

WORDS & MUSIC BY DOLLY PARTON

of you each step _____ of the way, _____ and
know that I'm not ____ what you need, _____ but } I _____ will

al - ways ___ love ___ you; _____ I ___ will al - - - ways ___ love ___

1.

you.

Bit - ter

2.

you.

Recite:
I hope that life treats you kind,
and I hope you have all that you ever dreamed of,
and I wish you joy and happiness,
but above all this, I wish you love.

Sing:
And I will always love you,
I will always love you,
I will always love you,
And I will always love you,
I will always love you,
I will always love you.

I'M KISSING YOU

LYRICS & MELODY BY DES'REE. MUSIC BY TIM ATACK

watch - ing stars_____ with-out__ you, My__ soul cried:_____

Heav - - - - ing heart____ is full____ of pain._____

Oh,_____ oh,_____ the ach - ing!_____ 'Cos

I'm_____ kiss - ing__ you,_____ oh._____

I'M YOUR ANGEL

WORDS & MUSIC BY R. KELLY

Verse 2:

R. KELLY: I saw your teardrops and I heard you crying
All you need is time, seek me and you shall find
You have everyting and you're still lonely
It don't have to be this way
Let me show you a better day

CELINE: And then you will see the morning will come
And all of your days will be bright as the sun
So all of your fears, just cast them on me
How can I make you see?

BOTH: I'll be your cloud *etc.*

JEALOUS GUY

WORDS & MUSIC BY JOHN LENNON

JUST THE TWO OF US

WORDS & MUSIC BY RALPH MACDONALD, WILLIAM SALTER & BILL WITHERS

(Now Dad this is a very sensitive subject)

(Just the two of us.) (Just the two of us.) 1. From the

first time the doc-tor placed you in my arms I knew— I'd meet death be-fore I'd let you meet harm. Al-though
(Verses 2 & 3 see block lyric)

ques-tions a - rose— in my mind, would I be man e - nough?— Against wrong choose right and be stand-in' up.

From the hos - pi - tal that first night took a hour just to get the car - seat in right.— Peo-ple

driv-in' all fast, got me kin-da up-set.— Got you home safe, placed you in your ba - son-ette. That

night I don't think one wink I slept— as I slipped— out my bed, to your crib I crept, touched your

head gent - ly, felt my heart melt 'cos I knew I loved you more that life it - self.— Then to my

knees, and I begged— the Lord "please let me be a good Dad- dy."— All he needs is

love, know - ledge, dis - ci - pline too. I pledge my life— to you. Just the

two of us,   we can make it if— we try.— Just the   two of us.————   (Just the

two   of us.)   *8va* - - - - -   Just——   the   two   of   us,————   build-ing   cas-

- tles   in—   the   sky.—   Just the   two   of   us,————   you and I.————   *8va* - - -

2, 3.

N.C.

And you can cry,   ain't no shame in it.   It did-n't work   out with me and your Mom.— But yo,

⊕ Coda

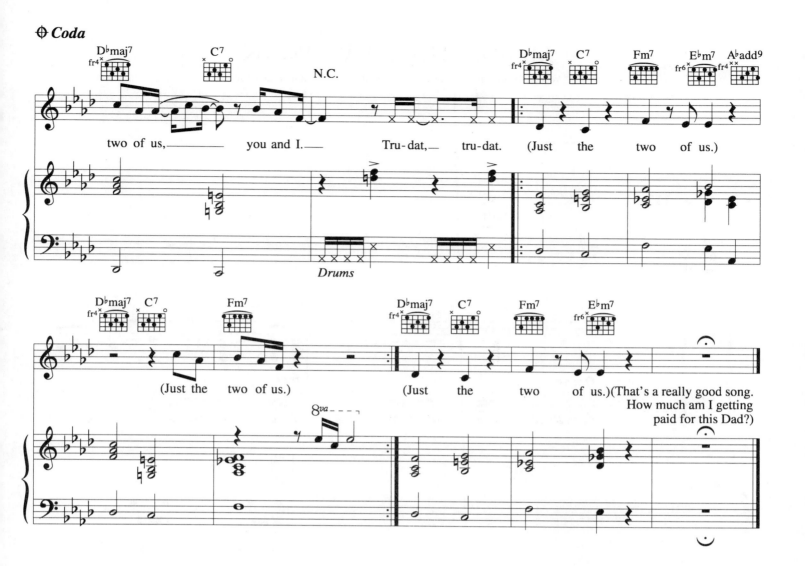

two of us,—— you and I.—— Tru-dat,— tru-dat. (Just the two of us.)

Drums

(Just the two of us.) (Just the two of us.)(That's a really good song. How much am I getting paid for this Dad?)

Verse 2:

Five years old, bringin' comedy
Everytime I look at you I think man, a little me
Just like me, wait and see gonna be tall
Makes me laugh cause you got your dad's ears and all
Sometimes I wonder, what you gonna be
A General, a Doctor, maybe a MC?
Haha, I wanna kiss you all the time
But I will test that butt when you cut outta line, trudat
Uh-uh-uh why do you do that?
I try to be a tough dad, but you be makin' me laugh
Crazy joy, when I see the eyes of my baby boy
I pledge to you, I will always do everything I can
Show you how to be a man
Dignity, integrity, honour and
I don't mind if you lose, long as you came with it
And you can cry, aint no shame in it
It didn't work out with me and your Mom
But yo, push come to shove, you was conceived in love
So if the world attacks, and you slide off track
Remember one fact, I got your back.

Just the two of us *etc.*

Verse 3:

It's a full-time job to be a good dad
You got so much more stuff than I had
I gotta study just to keep with the changin' times
101 Dalmations on your CD-ROM
See me, I'm tryin' to pretend I know
On my PC where dat CD go
But yo, ain't nuthin' promised, one day I'll be gone
Feel the strife, but trust life does go on
But just in case, it's my place to impart
One day some girl's gonna break your heart
And ooh ain't no pain like from the oppsite sex
Gonna hurt bad, but don't take it out on the next, son
Throughout life people will make you mad
Disrespect you and treat you bad
Let God deal with the things they do
Cause hate in your heart will consume you too
Always tell the truth, say your prayers
Hold doors, pull out chairs, easy on the swears
You're living proof that dreams come true
I love you and I'm here for you.

Just the two of us *etc.*

MORE THAN A WOMAN

WORDS & MUSIC BY BARRY GIBB, ROBIN GIBB & MAURICE GIBB

(Doo doo doo doo.)

(More than a wo - man.) (Doo doo doo doo.) 1. Oh,

girl I've known you ve - ry well, I've seen you grow-ing ev - 'ry day.— I
(Verse 2 see block lyric)

nev - er real - ly looked— be - fore.— (But now you take— my breath— a - way.—)

Sud-den - ly— you're in— my life,— part of ev - 'ry - thing— I do. You've

got me work - ing day— and— night. (Just try-ing to keep— a hold— on you.—)

(More than a wo - man.)   (Doo doo   doo doo.)   Oh yeah,_____

2.

(Doo doo   doo doo.)   (More than a wo - man.)
            Ooh, ba - by.

(Doo doo   doo doo.)
            Oh,_____   yeah,   yeah,   yeah._____

(More than a wo - man._____)   More than a wo - man.

78

Verse 2:
Oh yeah, there are stories old and true
Of people so in love like you and me
And I can see myself
(Let history repeat itself)
Reflecting how I feel for you
Think about those people then
I know that in a thousand years
(I'd fall in love with you again)
This is the only way that we should fly
This is the only way to go
And if I lose your love, I think I would die
Oh, say you'll always be my baby
We can make it shine
We can take forever just a minute at a time. Oh.

(More than a woman) *etc.*

MOONDANCE

WORDS & MUSIC BY VAN MORRISON

1. Well it's a mar - vel - lous night__ for a moon - dance, with the

(Verse 2 see block lyric; Verses 3-7 ad lib. instrumental)

To Coda ⊕

82

Can I just have one more moon-dance with you,

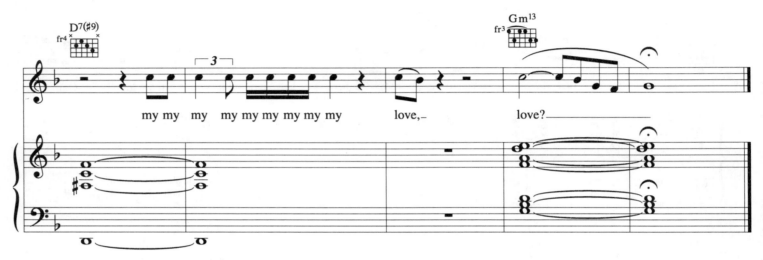

my my my my my my my my my love,— love?

Verse 2:

Well I wanna make love to you tonight,
I can't wait till the morning has come.
And I know now the timing is just right,
And straight into my arms you will run.
And when you come my heart will be waiting
To make sure that you're never alone.
There and then all my dreams will come true dear;
There and then I will make you my own.
Every time I touch you, you just tremble inside.
And I know how much I want you baby,
That you can't hide.
Can I just have one more moondance with you, my love?
Can I just make some more romance with you, my love?

MY ALL

MUSIC BY MARIAH CAREY & WALTER AFANSIEFF. WORDS BY MARIAH CAREY

NEVER EVER

WORDS & MUSIC BY SHAZNAY LEWIS. MUSIC BY RICKIDY RAW

or even on the phone, you can write it in a letter, either way I have to know. Did I never treat you right

did I always start the fight? Either way I'm going out of my mind, all the answers to my questions I have to find.

1. My head's spin - ning,— boy I'm in— a daze,— I feel i - so - lat - ed,
(Verse 2 see block lyric)

don't want to com - mun - i - cate.— I'll take a show-er, I will— scour,— I will run

Verse 2:
I keep searching deep within my soul
For all the answers, don't wanna hurt no more.
I need peace, got to feel at ease, need to be
Free from pain, go insane, my heart aches.

Sometimes vocabulary runs through my head
The alphabet runs right from A to Z
Conversations, hesitations in my mind.
You got my conscience asking questions that I can't find
I'm not crazy
I'm sure I ain't done nothing wrong
Now I'm just waiting
'Cause I heard that this feeling won't last that long.

THE POWER OF LOVE

WORDS & MUSIC BY C. DEROUGE, G. MENDE, J. RUSH & S. APPLEGATE

1. The whis-pers in the morn-ing
(Verse 2 see block lyric)

of lov-ers sleep-ing tight,

are roll-ing by like thun-der now

as I look in your eyes.

I hold on to your bo - dy,

and feel each move you make,

your voice is warm and ten - der, a love that

Verse 2:
Lost is how I'm feeling
Lying in your arms,
When the world outside's too much to take,
That all ends when I'm with you.
Even though there may be times
It seems I'm far away,
Never wonder where I am
'Cause I am always by your side.

SAVE THE BEST FOR LAST

WORDS & MUSIC BY JON LIND, WENDY WALDMAN & PHILIP GALDSTON

107

SO CLOSE

WORDS & MUSIC BY DINA CARROLL & NIGEL LOWIS

1. I've known a - bout all your faults, — some - how they nev - er de - ter — me, —
2. *(see block lyric)*

and there are times when we talk, — you real - ly know how to soothe

Verse 2:
Sometimes you say that I'm cold,
Don't ever think that you'll lose me.
I'll never tire of your hold,
'Cause you know just how to move me.
Well you're aware as I am too,
That there's good and bad in the things we do.
But after all is said and done,
There's nothing sweeter.

SOMEWHERE OUT THERE

WORDS & MUSIC BY JAMES HORNER, BARRY MANN & CYNTHIA WEIL

through,   then   we'll   be   to-geth   -   er   some-where   out   there,   out

where   dreams   come   true. _____

TAKE MY BREATH AWAY

WORDS BY TOM WHITLOCK. MUSIC BY GIORGIO MORODER

Watch-ing ev -'ry mo - tion in ___ my fool - ish lov - er's game; ___ on this end - less o - cean, fi -
Watch-ing, I keep wait - ing, still ___ an - tic - i - pat - ing love, ___ nev - er hes - i - tat - ing to ___
Watch-ing ev -'ry mo - tion in ___ this fool - ish lov - er's game; ___ haunt - ed by the no - tion some -

TRUE COLOURS

WORDS & MUSIC BY BILLY STEINBERG & TOM KELLY

123

Verse 2:
Show me a smile
Don't be unhappy
Can't remember when
I last saw you laughing
If this world makes you crazy
And you've taken all you can bear
Just call me up
Because you know I'll be there.

And I see your true colours *etc.*

UN-BREAK MY HEART

WORDS & MUSIC BY DIANE WARREN

WHAT CAN I DO

WORDS & MUSIC BY ANDREA CORR, CAROLINE CORR, SHARON CORR & JIM CORR

1. I have-n't slept— at all— in days;—
(Verse 3 see block lyric)

It's been so long— since we— have talked.—

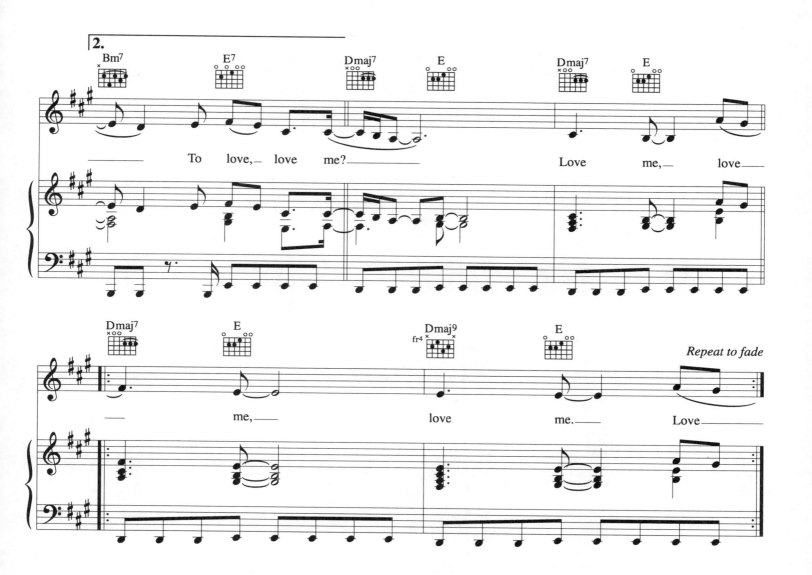

Verse 3:
Maybe there's nothing more to say;
And, in a funny way, I'm calm.
Because the power is not mine,
I'm just gonna let it fly.

WHEN YOU TELL ME THAT YOU LOVE ME

WORDS & MUSIC BY ALBERT HAMMOND & JOHN BETTIS

Moderate ballad

I wan-na call the stars down from the sky, I wan-na live a day that nev-er dies. I wan-na change the world on-ly for you, all the im-pos-si-ble I wan-na do. I wan-na

WHEN YOU'RE YOUNG AND IN LOVE

WORDS & MUSIC BY VAN McCOY

Verse 2:

The moon at night (Shines so bright)
Seems to shine twice as bright
When you're young and in love.

Dreams can come true (try a dream)
If you believe they do
When you're young and in love.

So many teardrops are bound to fall
True love can conquer all
When you're, when you're young and in love.

A WOMAN IN LOVE

WORDS & MUSIC BY BARRY GIBB & ROBIN GIBB

Life is a mo - ment in space, _____ when the dream is gone _____
With you e - ter - nal - ly mine, _____ in love there is _____

_____ it's a lone - li - er place. _____ I kiss the morn - ing good - bye, _____
_____ no mea - sure of time. _____ We planned it all at the start,

_____ but down in - - side _____ you know we nev - er know why.
_____ that you and I _____ live in each oth - er's heart.

It's a right _____ I de-fend, o-ver and o-ver a-gain. What do I do?

What do I do?

I am a wo-man in love _____ and I'm talk-in' to you.

YOU'RE STILL THE ONE

WORDS & MUSIC BY SHANIA TWAIN & ROBERT JOHN 'MUTT' LANGE

1. Looks like we made— it,———— look how far— we've come—
(Verse 2 see block lyric)

— my ba - by, we might have took the long— way,———

Verse 2:
Ain't nothing better
We beat the odds together
I'm glad we didn't listen
Look at what we would be missing.

They said, I bet,
They'll never make it
But just look at us holding on
We're still together, still going strong.

WHEN I NEED YOU

WORDS & MUSIC BY ALBERT HAMMOND & CAROLE BAYER SAGER

When I— need you, I just close my eyes and I'm
(Verse 3 see block lyric)

with you, and all that I so want to give you is on-ly a heart-beat a-way.— When I

Verse 2:
When I need you
I just close my eyes and I'm with you
And all that I so want to give you, baby
Is only a heartbeat away.

It's not easy when the road is your driver
But honey that's a heavy load that we bear.
But you know I won't be travelling a lifetime
It's cold out, but hold out and do like I do, oh I need you.

Verse 3: (D.𝄉.)
When I need love
I hold out my hands and I touch love
I never knew there was so much love
It's keeping me warm night and day.

I just hold out my hand… and I'm with you darling…
(To fade)

1/03(46470)